DEAR GIRL

You Are Special

Inspiring and Heartening Stories About

Courage, Friendship and Inner Strength to

Discover the Beauty of Being You

Motivational Gift-Book For Your Children

Written by

Kilye Watson

Contents

Introduction

You are unique. Always remember that.

When the whole world seems to be against you, when you feel that everyone is working against you, always remember that you are special and that no one else in the world is like you.

Especially at your age, losing self-esteem is very easy. Maybe the boy who teases you or your friends who don't like you can make you think you're wrong. But believe me, that's never the case.

In other words, if someone avoids you for no particular reason, you should avoid them. This means that they are not right for you and you will certainly find someone who understands you.

If you think about it, it's perfectly normal to find people you don't like. I think you'll have some friends you want to spend all your time with and some you'll hate being with.

We are not all the same, and each of us has the

right to choose who to date and who not to date.

So if someone doesn't want to be with you, don't worry, it's normal. Life goes on, and you will surely find someone who is right for you.

But that's just one of the problems you may encounter at this age.

I have met many girls who have lost their self-esteem for different reasons: a bad grade, fear of going home alone, not believing in their dreams, etc.

In the next chapters, we will tell you real-life stories of people your age (or similar) who have overcome their fears and insecurities after realizing that they are unique.

What about you? Do you know that you are unique?

If you're still not convinced, read all the following stories; they'll do you good and improve your life.

Enjoy your reading!

The Fear Of
The End-Of-Year Show

"Mom, but I don't want to go!".

Little Greta sits sullenly on the bed, her long brown hair covering her face.

"Greta, you know very well that you still have to go. The end-of-year show is and will be a big deal for you. You know everyone will be there."

Her mom sits next to her and shakes her hair a bit, looking intently into her big green eyes.

"But I am not good at acting, and I don't like it at all. I told you I always forget every word I have to say."

To be honest, last year's performance was not a happy memory for Greta - she would have preferred to forget about it completely. Unfortunately, as happens to many boys and girls at the end of elementary school, she stood on the stage unable to say a word for nearly five interminable minutes before her beloved teacher came to her rescue.

Therefore, her mother knew very well that Greta was terrified that this sad scene would happen again.

"Greta, you have to understand that the year-end show is not a competition. No one cares who is the best or the most talented, it's just one of the many ways we can all be happy together at the end of the year" after those words, she smiles to encourage him.

There are still three months to go before the play begins and all the boys, girls, and mistresses are getting ready.

However, the day the teacher would decide to assign the different roles in the play to the whole class had arrived, so then the rehearsals could begin until the big day that Greta hated.

Apart from her, the end-of-year theater performance is the most awaited moment for all the students and, in fact, her classmates have always competed for the role of the protagonist while she, little Greta, has the desire to play a simple tree so that she can stand still without having to say a single word.

"Great, kids! It's time to assign roles for the play," the teacher said, adjusting her glasses on her nose and beginning to call out the students' names in alphabetical order.

After the teacher's words, some of Greta's classmates are delighted to be given a very important role, while others are a little angry because they are not happy with the role they have been given.

Much to her relief, Greta is given the role of a mere extra.

Everything seems to be solved, but during the rehearsals, the first little problems start to happen to her. After each sentence, Greta is blocked and unable to speak.

"Don't worry, Greta. There's no need to learn the text by heart. You can just read it."

So the teacher comes up on stage next to her and tries to help her: "What's got you so upset? Boys and girls, let's sit for a moment here on the stage, all in a circle, this can be a helpful moment for all of you. It can happen to everyone to be stuck or even afraid, and we have to try to solve this little problem together.

The players all come on stage and begin to form a large circle.

"It's just that I'm terrified of making another bad impression. I know perfectly well that I'm not good at acting. I imagine standing in front of so many other people and not being able to say anything," Greta says.

She explains to the class that fear is blocking her, but not only that. And also the strong conviction that she is not that good and that she will make a bad impression in front of the audience.

"Fear should encourage us to get better, kids, but it shouldn't become a big obstacle." The teacher then looks into Greta's big green eyes and smiles sweetly, "We're all good at something and not so good at something else. Our show is beautiful the way it is, even if the truth is that it won't be perfect. And you should know that many parents have told me that it's beautiful, mostly because someone often forgets the words because someone else is yelling or talking too fast, and we can't understand anything they say."

Upon hearing these words, everyone laughs as they watch Federica, a little girl with braces. And she starts to laugh too.

That afternoon, much to her mother's relief, Greta went home with a big smile and feeling even more relieved.

Realizing that her classmates almost never judged her was a very positive thing.

For a few weeks after that day, everything seemed to be going well, she could almost make her speech without getting stuck and never forgot the words to say. However, as the day of the play approached, her fears began to surface.

The last rehearsals, as she expected, are a disaster, and a few days before the performance, Greta finds herself on stage without being able to say a single word. She is sad, certain that everything will go wrong like last year.

"Greta," someone calls to her from behind the stage. She sits nervously backstage and watches her carefree classmates rehearse. She turns around and still sees Federica, the little girl with braces, coming toward her.

"Greta, I have a great idea!" She looks at her in puzzlement. "You're very good at singing, I've heard you once!" Greta, although pleased with the compliment, still doesn't understand, "Well, I don't know if I'm very good...but I like to sing."

Federica smiles at her: "And I'm telling you that you are very good! Even our music teacher confirmed that you are one of the best in the school! So why don't you try singing your whole part instead of acting? If you learn it by singing, it will be much easier for you to play it!"

Greta looks at her with surprise. This is a spectacular idea!

"But how can I sing it without a musical base?" "I'll take care of it, don't worry," Federica smiled at him again.

The next afternoon, Federica, accompanied by her mother, showed up at Greta's house with a guitar on her shoulders.

"You can play the guitar too," Greta asks him excitedly. "Actually, only a few songs, but I think we can still try. They spend the afternoon in the garden, sitting under a big tree, playing and singing happily.

Greta discovers many things about Federica. She discovers that she has been playing the guitar since she received her famous braces two years ago. She discovers that for a long time she was ashamed of speaking fast and that she tried to improve her pronunciation of words by singing.

"Singing, among other things, has taught me to speak more slowly! I was also terrified of public speaking until a few months ago. I was afraid that people would laugh at me because I sometimes speak so fast that people don't understand what I'm saying.

Federica laughs and her large braces shine in the sunlight.

"Singing has helped me a lot. That's why I thought all this might help you too!" And, in fact, she was right.

The next day, during the long-awaited final rehearsal, Greta managed not to make a mistake. Not a single word.

In her head, she imagined that she was singing the song and, in the meantime, she could also recite the words. The speech was perfect. With all the pauses at the right times, not too fast, not too slow.

The teacher congratulated her several times, and Federica always winked at her from the sidelines.

It worked! Using music to memorize words finally worked! Greta finally fell asleep much more serenely than usual.

For the first time, she has the feeling that the much-hated show is going to go very well.

Her mother can breathe a big sigh of relief, seeing her so relaxed. Everything is now ready. The curtain falls and all her classmates, following the script, enter the stage. When it's her turn, Greta takes a deep breath and steps on stage.

The teacher in the front row looks at her and makes a gesture of affection to encourage her.

Behind her, all the parents are sitting, smiling and silent, staring at her. Greta laughs, the beloved song she learned with Federica rings in her head, and she begins to recite the words perfectly. One after the other. Without making a single mistake.

And it will be a great success!

"You were unique, Greta!", Federica compliments her backstage. "Thanks, Fede, you helped me a lot!". "This will remain our secret," they both smile and crouch down together to enjoy the rest of the show, as if they were two friends who had been dating for a long time.

Sometimes fears can immobilize us and seem insurmountable, but we must remember that there is always a solution.

It is often our talents (everyone has many) that help us succeed, even in the most difficult times.

Have you ever felt like running away from something that terrifies you? Or feel uncomfortable in a certain situation at school, with your family or friends?

What are some of the things you're afraid of right now?

We all face fears in our lives, and each of us has our own time and way of dealing with them. It's really nothing to be ashamed of. On the contrary, when we realize that we are afraid of something, our journey of growth and problem-solving begins.

Everyday life presents us with challenges, big and small, that we need in order to grow.

After all, every fear is nothing more than a challenge to ourselves!

Marta's Vacations

"I'll get it, Dad."

Marta runs to the sea to catch the ball that has rolled to where the water begins. She has always loved to feel warm, almost burning sand under her little feet. Marta loves all vacations. Getting up very late in the morning, and spending whole afternoons at the beach, going for walks in the evening with her parents and her little sister. There is nothing she doesn't like on vacation!

Well, almost.

In fact, there's one small thing that's important: for some strange reason, Marta has a hard time making friends.

"Pass Marta, pass it!" her sister Annachiara, only four years old, makes many signs to throw the ball to her. Marta and Annachiara are madly in love with each other, although, like all sisters, they don't always get along. Marta is often annoyed that Annachiara has so many friends that she does not.

That afternoon it was very hot and Marta's mother joined her husband and two little girls with four wonderful fresh granites.

"Come on, it's time to cool off a bit. You've been playing for almost two hours!"

Marta goes to her mother and immediately notices that there is only one mint slushie, the one with the green color, obviously.

Mint has always been her favorite flavor, but it's also her sister Annachiara's favorite flavor! So while Annachiara puts the balloon under the umbrella, Marta immediately grabs the glass filled with green granite and starts eating it eagerly.

"This is delicious, Mom!"

"But mom, that's not fair! She got the mint slushie! I wanted it too!" Annachiara, with eyes full of tears, looks at Marta as she enjoys the green granite. Marta looks very satisfied because she thinks she was right to get her favorite flavor.

Happy and serene, she lies down on the mattress under the umbrella and starts sipping her granite, pretending not to listen to Annachiara who is crying nearby. In the early afternoon, the two sisters decide to play some of the games offered daily by the animation service.

There are also many other boys and girls.

The animators explain a game with prizes, and the winner receives an ice cream and also a free entrance to the zoo with the animators.

The game consists of a sequence of two-person races, with the winners competing in subsequent races until only one team is left to win it all.

Marta looks around, her sister Annachiara is too young to win, she certainly can't compete with her!

She takes a quick look at everyone present and immediately sees a rather tall guy.

"He sounds like a very strong boy. I must be on his team!" she thinks.

In 15 minutes, the couples are all formed. Marta teams up with Ivan, this tall guy. Annachiara, on the other hand, teams up with a little girl with curly red hair.

The first race is a slightly modified race. One of the facilitators ties one of Marta's wrists to one of Ivan's wrists because they have to run together.

"OK, now we have to win," Marta says proudly. The race begins. Marta and Ivan immediately prove that they are the strongest, as they run very fast. They are the first, but at one point, Ivan stumbles and falls to the ground. Marta pulls him with her wrist, urging him to get up, but he holds his ankle and does not get up. The other couples join them and if Ivan does not get up, they will be overtaken and eliminated!

Without thinking more than once, Marta untied the knot that bound them and began to run again, practically alone.

She leaves Ivan on the ground and reaches the finish line. She is first!

In the second competition, Marta is given a new

partner. Her name is Miriam.

She is tall with a face full of freckles. In this new event, the competitors have to swim in the children's pool.

The fastest couple wins.

Unfortunately for Marta, Miriam is not a good swimmer at all. They manage not to lose the heat but finish in the last positions.

Before the beginning of the third competition, Marta goes to the host.

"I want to change partners!" she said with determination. "Why? What's wrong with Miriam?" the boy asks. "Miriam is too slow. She makes me lose too many points."

The host looks at her unconvinced and says, "Unfortunately, this is a two-person contest, Marta. You have to play with your designated partner."

"I don't care! I want to change partners! Or I'll race by myself!" After an endless series of tantrums, the host finally allowed Marta to compete alone.

The third race is a classic obstacle course. Marta, playing alone, arrives first. Annachiara's partner, however, falls during the course. Instead of continuing and leaving her on the ground, Annachiara stops with her and even helps her up.

Together they go to the host's station, who has meanwhile found a bag of ice. Unfortunately, the curly-haired girl can no longer compete, but Annachiara is fortunately not disqualified.

Her beautiful gesture of help was so appreciated by the hosts that they unanimously decided not to eliminate her from the competition and to assign her a new partner. Annachiara's new partner was Miriam, who had been left alone in the meantime, waiting for someone to replace her.

The races continue and the two sisters manage to

stay in the game.

It's time for the very last competition: the high jump. Annachiara is small, and her score is, of course, very low, but Miriam is a real phenomenon in the high jump, and together they manage to come first. And her sister, Marta, came second.

"Miriam and Annachiara win an ice cream and free admission to the zoo! Congratulations girls!", the hosts decide to accompany the winners to the ice cream shop.

Marta addresses the host from before: "It's not fair! I had to compete alone! You have to take that into account too! If I had had a partner, I would have won for sure!" she says with bitterness.

"Marta, you're the one who didn't want a boyfriend or girlfriend. You were on Miriam's team, remember? It was you who asked to compete alone," the host replied.

"But I didn't know Miriam was so good at the high jump! In fact, I didn't even know there was going to be a high jump competition for couples. If I had known, of course, I would have stayed with her!" she says, with tears in her eyes.

Marta can't stand losing, especially to her sister. The host smiles at her and invites her to sit on a bench.

"I deserved to win!" continues Marta, crying. "My sister is much worse than me, it's not fair that she won!"

The host shakes his head: "No, Marta. Your sister played honestly. She helped her partner when she was injured, even at the cost of losing the match. And she didn't complain when her partner was not as good as her. You, on the other hand, left Ivan on the floor, in pain, and continued on your own, even asking to remove Miriam from your team. You see, Marta, you can't just think about yourself. You can't always receive favors and never give anything back. I'm sorry, but your sister deserves to win more than you do. She won, and she also found a friend."

That night, something strange happened.

When dinner was over, Marta let Annachiara have the last piece of chocolate cake. Without making a face or throwing a tantrum.

She took the plate and pushed it affectionately towards her sister, showing a big smile.

From that day on, Marta never had a mint slushy first and had no trouble making friends.

Before that day, she had always thought that doing something for others was a sign of weakness; instead, she understood that life is not only about receiving but especially about giving!

What about you? Do you consider yourself more like Marta or Annachiara?

We often find ourselves in great difficulty when we have to do something for others, we always start thinking about convenience.

Should I help my friend or not? What's in it for me?

But I tell you that acting only in your own interests never leads to anything. On the contrary, it is only by spontaneously helping others that we can receive their sincere affection.

Would you like someone (friend or acquaintance) to consider whether it would be right for them before helping you?

That is why the gesture made with sincerity is the most important: make one sincere gesture, and you will receive a thousand in response.

Height Is Just A Number

"Emily, are you ready? In less than 10 minutes, all your friends are going to arrive," the mom enters the room and finds Emily still lying on the bed.

It's now summer, vacation has been underway for about a month, and twice a week Emily and a few of the kids gather in the morning in the yard downstairs to play soccer.

"I don't want to go today, Mom. Emily turns away and goes back to sleep. "Why do you say that? Don't you like playing with all your friends anymore?" the pensive-looking mom sits down next to her, worried.

"No. I don't feel like it today."

"Why? What happened? Did you have a fight?"

In fact, it's always the same story for Emily, when the boys are divided into two teams to play basketball, she is always avoided and then chosen last.

But it's not because she's not good, on the contrary, Emily is very athletic and very sporty, but genetically, she is rather small. Emily's friends are very competitive and unfortunately for her, because of her size, she has trouble shooting the ball in the basket.

"I'm too small for basketball, Mom. No one wants me on the team anymore."

Emily hugs the pillow again and sighs deeply. "Oh, Emily. There's more to life than basketball for the rest of us. Who says it's better to be the tall one all the time?"

Emily turns to her mother. "Of course, it's always better to be tall! It's a big advantage for all the things we do! And I'm too small actually, I'm the smallest," she hits the pillow hard in a very nervous way.

"Emily, you have to understand that we are all different. In the world, there are big people and small people, and there is nothing wrong with that. Everyone is good at some things and not so good at others... Maybe in basketball, your friends don't pick you like they used to, but in many other occasions, they would. And that's just the way it is," and she smiles sweetly at him.

"Come on, get ready, they'll be here any minute." Emily grinned in disappointment and stood up, "There are ten of us after all, so we have to make two teams of five."

The children are all gathered in the courtyard and are already starting to organize their teams. The captains for this morning are Alfonso and Betty. Emily looks at Betty and feels a little envious because she wishes she had legs as long and thin as Betty's!

Betty is very tall, muscular, and can practically be described as the perfect girl to play basketball with! In fact, everyone wants her on the team all the time.

In a few minutes, the boys choose their team members and, as expected, Emily is chosen last. She is on Betty's team.

They start playing and Emily feels almost invisible. No one passes her the ball, and if they do, it's only because there's no alternative.

This makes her very sad. Because of her size, she is excluded from the game and is not considered by her friends.

How she wishes she were taller! "Look out!" Alfonso attempted a basket, but the ball hit the rim and bounced.

The ball bounces off the ground, rolls a few feet toward the nearby porch, and then slips through Emily's neighbor's door. "Oh no," Alfonso looks in amazement at where the ball disappeared, "who's going to get it back now from the crazy psychologist?" he laughs.

"I'm going to go," Emily heads for the door, "I've known Dr. Della Corte since I was a little girl. Hold on a second."

She knocks gently and enters her neighbor's house.

"Dr. Della Corte"? Excuse me? May I?" She looks around. She had never been inside Dr. Della Corte's house before. He's an elderly psychologist looks rather cheerful, the neighbors say he's a little crazy, but Emily always thought he was nice.

"Emily, dear, what are you doing here?" The doctor arrives, a book in his hands and old-fashioned glasses on his nose. "Hello Doctor, I beg your pardon, we were playing with the ball, and it accidentally got in here in your house. The door was ajar..." Emily tries to explain to the doctor.

"There's something troubling you, my friend. Please sit down and tell me all about it," the doctor takes a comfortable chair and pushes it towards Emily. It was only after this movement that the girl noticed the mess that covered the house. Maybe the doctor really was a little crazy after all.

"No, thanks doctor, I'm fine, I just came here for the ball." But he stares at her from behind his glasses, as if trying to unlock a secret, "Dear Emily, I've been analyzing people for many years, it's the job I love. I know when something is wrong. And in you, I can bet as much as you want that there is something wrong", he signals her again to sit down.

A little impressed with his calm words and also eager to talk about her problems with someone, Emily settled down, "OK." Within minutes, Emily explained to Dr. Della Corte about her size problem.

She would like to be taller, be liked by her friends, and be better at basketball. "Fortunately," the doctor said with a big smile, "all of that is largely possible! It would have been much more complicated if you had told me you wanted to fly," she laughed. "How would that be possible? You mean I can grow up if I want to?", Emily's heart flutters.

"No, kiddo, unfortunately, height is not up to us, so we can't change it, but many other things can! The real problem is not that you want to get taller, you just want your friends to like you more, and you think that being taller will help you. You're convinced that if you were taller, you'd play better basketball and your friends would like you more. No ?"

Emily nodded her head in agreement. In fact, think about it, if you were tall, but still not good at basketball, your friends wouldn't consider you! So, at the end of the day, your problem is definitely not height.

The problem is basketball. You want to be good at basketball because you want your friends to consider you." Emily stared at him without saying a word.

How had he figured out all these things in so few minutes?

"And the solution is very simple: you have to play good basketball! "The doctor looks at her with satisfaction.

"That's another big problem, Doctor. How can I play basketball well if I'm so small? I can't compete with all my tall friends," Emily tells him.

"You certainly can't compete in size, but you can compete in speed, where you'd be the best," the doctor winks at her, gets up, and quietly heads into the other room, his book in hand.

"It's about time! Did you also have a hot tea while you were waiting?" his friends laughed. Their wait was much longer than expected.

"I always said that psychologist was crazy," Alfonso laughs. The boys get back into the game and this time Emily really surprises everyone.

Following Dr. Della Corte's advice, she refrains from shooting the ball in the basket, but uses her light and short physique to run nimbly between opponents.

"And when did you learn that?", Alfonso looks at her in surprise as she dashes to the basket, leaving all the opponents behind.

"Pass Emily! " Betty, a few steps from the basket, steals the ball and scores the winning points.

No one is faster than her! She can easily dodge anyone in front of her, carries the ball to the shooting area, and passes it perfectly to her classmates who score and rejoice.

Since that day, almost everyone wants Emily on their team, and being small is her biggest advantage!

With her new skill, she has earned the respect and even the total consideration of virtually the entire group.

Each of us has specific qualities, and sometimes you just have to look at things from a different angle to see all the positive sides.

Our beauty begins to manifest itself the moment we start to accept ourselves as we are: when Emily stopped wishing she were tall, she realized all the advantages her size (or smallness) offered her!

Is there anything about your appearance or character that you don't like and would like to change? What is the reason for this? Often we would like to change these things in ourselves to be more appreciated by our friends and acquaintances because we want to be accepted and appreciated by others.

In reality, it is simple enough to be able to accept ourselves, as we were created, then all our infinite potential manifests itself with others!

You Don't Have To Be
A Hero To Have Courage

Antoinette was in her room reading the story of a hero who, in his quest for a rich treasure, found himself fighting fierce dragons, crossing dangerous rivers, having to defeat evil witches, and overcoming a thousand other adventures that required incredible courage and unusual abilities.

"I will never succeed in becoming a hero, I don't have enough courage to face complicated or even threatening situations. Besides, I don't think I have any talent at all, I'm just an ordinary little girl who is nothing special," she reflects in her mind, with much regret, as the corners of her little mouth start to curve down more and more, like when she feels like crying.

She didn't complain about her life: Antoinette went to school all the time, loved to study, practiced hip-hop dance, and had a lot of fun with her dear friend Angelica, who lived just a few meters away from her home.

At school, besides Angelica, she sometimes talked to other girls or boys, but she often thought that few people knew her at school, and she was not popular.

And today, when the weather was as dark as the clouds that filled the sky, she felt like her presence (or even absence) at school didn't make much of a difference.

"I admit it: I don't have the audacity of Chiaretta, who always seems so sure of herself by always having her gang around her. I'm not as funny as Gianni, who always makes jokes and makes everyone smile; nor am I as stressful as Gianmario, who admittedly is often annoying, but is certainly someone who gets noticed. No one notices me like I'm invisible," she thought to herself, frowning more and more.

Finally, with a heavy sigh, she decided to take the book away and go to Angelica's house, in order to distract herself a little from her awful sad thoughts and try to change the completely negative mood that surrounded her.

"Antoinette, how about we make a cake for tonight?" her sweet mom asks as she walks into the kitchen. "Mom, I'm going to go see Angelica for a bit, it's been a long time since we've seen each other after finishing our homework," says Antonietta.

"Okay, love, but try to be back in an hour or so, until it's dark. And remember the umbrella," the mother said.

"Yeah, no problem," Antoinette replies as she slips on her sneakers and heads outside. She liked where she lived, there were lots of small, low houses and lots of green space. Angelica's house was at the other end of the street, where there were stores.

With rain in the forecast, there was hardly anyone on the street at the time. Except for three children of his own age who were talking in a very agitated manner.

As she walked around and approached, Antoinette recognized Mohammed, the couple's son who had opened a kebab and pizza store a few yards away.

Mohammed was in the same school as her, even though he was smaller.

Among other things, apart from his age, he was also smaller in stature, shorter and thinner.

"Give me a bike, you African!" the older of the two boys present yelled at him with a super threatening look.

"But no, I'm not African, I'm Turkish!" replies Mohammed in a frightened voice. "But yes, it's the same thing! You don't even know how to speak our language!" says the older boy, with a mocking tone.

"I told you, you had to give me the bike!" he added even more authoritatively.

"But I can't, it's a gift from my father, I need it to go to school" Mohammed replied, trying to resist, but his face looked more and more terrified. Antonietta, who had understood the situation well, quickly thought of how to save Mohammed from the wrath of the two criminals.

"I need to get someone to help me right now!" she thought to herself as she looked down the deserted street.

Fortunately, Alfredino's grandfather, the child who lived across the street from her, was leaving the house at that very moment. Antonietta ran to him and explained what was going on.

"Quick, let's run to help Mohammed!" said the grandfather as soon as Antoinette finished her story. One of the two young boys held Mohammed tightly and the other held his bike.

"Stop it! What are you doing?" exclaimed Alfredino's grandfather. "But nothing sir, we were just joking with our Moroccan friend," said the older one to justify himself, while the younger one did not raise his head and moved his shoe from left to right as if he wanted to move a non-existent pebble.

"But what would your parents say if they found you doing something like this? I really don't think that's what you were taught, and I'm sure you wouldn't behave like that in front of them! But is it right to steal a child's bike? Do you know that it is, among other things, a crime that is severely punished by the law?" exclaimed the very angry grandfather.

The older boy, not at all expecting to be caught in the act, lost all the courage he had up to that point and stammered, "I... I don't know...we didn't mean to." Antoinette, furious at what had happened, pointed her umbrella at him and shouted, "Shame on you! You fought two against one! You are cowards! But didn't you think how much you would have frightened Mohammed with your ugly threats? And if any of you had been in his place, how would you have felt?"

Both children were now as red in the face as peppers and could not lift their heads or look at the ground.

The smaller one, after a few moments, even began to whimper. "But I didn't mean to do it," he said in a soft voice.

"As Antoinette said, before you take these actions against someone else, try to put yourself in their shoes and think about how you might feel. Remember that 'Never do unto others what you would not want to be done to you', is always a very good rule to follow," Grandpa repeated.

"Bullism is not at all the behavior of the strong, but rather of the weak. There is nothing heroic about bullying defenseless people. And those who do not directly participate and do nothing to help the current victim of bullies are just as responsible," the grandfather added.

"It's time to shake hands with Mohammed and apologize," he told them. "Excuse us," "Sorry Mohammed," the two children shouted, sincerely repentant.

"Now go home and never do anything like that again!".

"Dear Antoinette, you have been very brave! " Said the grandfather, placing his hands on her shoulders with great affection. "And you did very well to ask for help from an adult so that you could resolve this complicated situation," he told her with a smile.

Antoinette, who thought she could be anything but brave, admitted that yes, she really was! And it feels good to help someone in need!

"Thank you, Antoinette," Mohammed murmured with a beaming smile, "You are my hero now!".

"Actually, we call her my hero, because she is a woman, but yes, Antoinette, you will be a hero to me too from now on," Grandpa said with infinite sweetness.

Mohammed asked the two to accompany him to his parents' store and when he had finished telling them everything that had happened, the parents gave a tray full of Turkish sweets to the two "saviors of their son" as a sign of gratitude.

Antoinette, after a few exchanges, went home, happy with the way things had gone and also with the fact that she had managed to bring back a nice tray of cakes for dinner, as she had not made a cake with her mom.

Unlike the other days, when dark thoughts had invaded her and lowered her mood, Antoinette was now feeling very good.

An infinite feeling of well-being fills her heart, and she reflects on the fact that it is not necessary to perform extraordinary actions to be considered a hero, but that one can really become one in everyday life, contributing to the well-being of others and improving the surrounding reality.

Does The Monster
On The Way Home Exist?

Little Sonia was growing up. She was in the fourth grade at the school in her village where she had lived since birth.

Sonia loved going to school. She loved her teachers, her friends and even the janitors who looked after her class. She was perhaps one of the few children in the world who, when the alarm clock went off in the morning, instead of wanting to go back to sleep, was happy to be able to go to school.

The new year had started well as usual: the usual friendships, the usual passion and a lot of fun.

Little Sonia, however, did not know that on that October day, everything would change.

The mother had not worked since her delivery, since her little brother, Luca, was born three years later.

But that day, as the whole family is at the dinner table, she says, "Do you want to hear the good news?" "Of course mom!" reply Sonia and Luca in unison.

"Starting Monday, I will finally go back to work!"

The whole family began to rejoice, and they all started to sing a song.

While she was singing, Sonia started thinking about one thing: What kind of hours would Mom make?

She immediately asked. "I'll be working from 9 am to 4 pm sweetie, so first I'll drive you to school, and then I'll go."

Sonia began to realize that one of her nightmares was about to become reality.

"What about the ride home?" she said in an anxious voice. "On the way home, I'll pick up Luca, because he leaves at 4:30, while you... you're a big girl now. When you leave at 2 pm, you can walk home, it's only a few hundred meters after all."

Sonia lost the color on her face. She had always been terrified of walking this path alone and now, out of necessity, she would be forced to.

"Maybe I can wait for Luca to get out of school too!" she hinted. "You can't stay there for more than two hours, Sonia. But what's on your mind?"

mom asked gently. "Nothing, Mom. I just have to get used to it."

Sonia said this sentence to reassure her parents, but deep down she knew that she would not be able to overcome her enormous fear.

After dinner, she went to her room, lay down on her bed, and started thinking about Monday. Since she was four years old, she had always seen this street as a labyrinth full of traps.

Why? Because at that time, something quite unusual had happened in his village.

A known criminal had escaped from the prison a few miles away. He was famous for kidnapping girls and demanding a ransom. Of course, as the news spread, stories and legends grew. Everyone claimed to have seen him, and one night even Sonia's neighbors said they saw the criminal running past their house.

Since that day, Sonia, small and impressionable,

was convinced that the thief (who had never actually been there) could still be in that street.

She began to imagine all the possible hiding places for this criminal on the way home from school. She tried to think of all the trees she had to get away from, all the bushes, all the garbage cans. Anyway, after a few minutes, she figured there was no way she could make that trip alone.

As always, everything is amplified in the minds of people (especially children).

Sonia should have covered a maximum of 250 meters at the end of the day, almost half of which with her friend Elvira.

Monday came and Sonia tried to convince her mother that she had a fever. Then her mother took the thermometer, but nothing: 36.2.

Sonia should have gone to school.

After the bell, the little girl just looked at her

watch. Every minute that passed was like a blow to the heart: the time to go home was getting closer and closer.

The last hour was coming to an end and the master, noticing the terror in Sonia's eyes, asked her what was going on.

"Nothing sir, I'm not feeling very well, I'm looking forward to going home."

The bell announcing the end of classes rang and Sonia, after some procrastination and discussion with her friends, found herself with Elvira on the way home.

Although it was a day with perfect weather, neither hot nor cold, Sonia started to sweat like she was running a marathon in August.

The first trip, the one we made together, was easy enough that Elvira did not even notice her anxiety. However, when she arrived at her friend's house, she realized that from that moment on she would have to walk alone, and she let out a loud cry.

However, she did not say anything about her fear. She only mentioned that she didn't feel well, so Elvira took her into the house.

She sat on Elvira's couch for two hours until her mother, back from her first day of work, came to pick her up (also a little worried).

As soon as she saw her mom's car, everything seemed to disappear. She waved and thanked Elvira and her parents, and within seconds she was sitting in her mom's car.

"What's wrong with you, love?" said the mother apprehensively. "Nothing, mom, now it's over."

The mother realized that something was wrong, but she preferred not to say more and to talk about it calmly at home.

After dinner, after putting Luca to bed, Sonia was on her bed thinking of what excuse she could make up for the next day. Mom looked at her for a few seconds and, seeing her concern, intervened, "Baby, now you have to tell me what's bothering you." "It's okay mom, don't worry. I'm fine now," Sonia said. "That's not true, I know you, there's something that's bothering you so much, and I want to know what it is" the mom repeated. "But mom, it's not a big deal, it's just that today I wasn't feeling well, and I was afraid I would get sick walking alone. But tomorrow will be better."

The mother tried to trust her daughter and, after a goodnight kiss, returned to her room.

Sonia slept with difficulty. Now that she had said that everything was fine the next day, she would have no excuse to use it: she had to go home alone.

And here is the morning: breakfast, backpack, and departure for school.

Her mother, busy with her new job, did not notice Sonia's growing concern, as she felt increasingly lonely and scared.

They finished their lessons and together with Elvira they went home. When they reached the point where they had to separate, Sonia hesitated. "Are you still sick? Should I call mom?" "No, Elvi, I'm fine, I just need to find the courage," Sonia said softly. "Courage to do what?" "To go home alone."

The best friend was puzzled for a moment. On the other hand, she didn't understand how walking alone for a hundred meters could scare Sonia so much.

"What are you afraid of? It's always the same road!"

"You want to know the truth? I'm convinced that the criminal who kidnapped the little girls, the one we've been talking about on TV, is still hiding somewhere along the way, remember?"

"Of course! But after all these years, it's not possible that he's still there hiding. He would have starved to death, wouldn't he?" said Elvira.

Indeed, Elvira's reasoning was sound. Where had he eaten all these years? Where had he bathed? And most importantly, where had he gone to the bathroom?

However, despite everything, Sonia was as if paralyzed. Her friend had a good idea: "I'll accompany you home today, so you'll see that there's nothing to fear on the way back and that, above all, I'll be able to get home safely on my own.

Sonia sighed with relief and hugged her friend. Together they arrived home quietly, and indeed, nothing had happened.

They hugged again and Elvira went home alone.

After eating, Sonia was on the bed and, for no apparent reason, wondered if something had happened to her friend on the way home.

Fear overcame the girl, and she had to run to her

parents, begging them to call her friend's parents to see if she was okay. After a few refusals, the mother called her friend's parents.

Elvira was sleeping in her room.

Sonia was able to fall asleep a little more peacefully.

The next day, as we left school, our protagonist seemed to have convinced herself that the short trip from home to school was safe.

They arrived again at the point where they had to separate.

"Sonia, do you want me to go with you today too?" her friend asks. "No, Elvi, thank you. I realized yesterday that there is nothing to worry about. I will do it alone."

The two of them say goodbye and leave, Sonia goes to her house.

After a few meters, she started to look around and

everything seemed normal. There was a long line of houses similar to hers, and the only things that were out of place were a few fallen railings, maybe because of the strong wind of the last few days.

But the first unexpected event happened. Behind a large trash can, she heard a noise, something moving.

"It's him, he waited until I was alone to kidnap me!" thought Sonia.

She remained petrified for a few moments until, to her great relief, she saw a tail wagging behind the trash can: it was a cat looking for food.

Relieved, she continued her walk.

After a few meters, another problem arose. A large, thick bush was moving, making suspicious noises. Sonia hoped it was more cats, but this time no tails came out.

This time she was sure: the criminal was about to

kidnap her.

Fear clouded her mind so much that she picked up a small stone and threw it toward the bush.

To his surprise, no criminals came out, only two birds that may have been building their nests.

Sonia felt a little guilty, but her attention immediately turned to the last few meters to go. They were the ones that terrified her the most because she would have to pass under the house of her neighbors who had said they had seen the criminal.

In her mind, she had always been convinced that he was just there, waiting to kidnap her.

After a few moments of hesitation, she took courage and, almost running, crossed this obstacle and finally arrived at her home.

Sonia was thrilled. Everything had gone well and, most importantly, she had overcome what was perhaps her greatest fear.

In the evening, while having dinner with her family, Sonia found the courage to talk to her parents about her fear and told them everything: she confessed to her aches and pains of the last few days and told them about her "adventure" in solitude on the way home.

Sonia's father and mother were proud of their daughter's courage, but wanted to make one thing clear:

"Baby, we are proud of you and your courage. Overcoming fears is never easy. We adults usually can't do it at all anymore, and we carry them with us all our lives.

However, always remember that on the street, you should NEVER trust strangers. You should only talk to people you know, and you should NEVER follow people you have never seen before."

"No, honey, this person was found years ago in a small town far from here. Didn't you know that?" said the mom.

"Wow, no, I didn't know that. If I had known, my fear would never have existed!" cried Sonia.

"Honey, look on the bright side: now you know you're strong enough to overcome your fears on your own. Of course, next time you better ask for our help, we're always with you."

"Okay mom, but now I'm not afraid. But as you say, I'm still going to be wary of strangers."

"Bravo, my daughter, your father and I are proud of you! " Said the mother smiling.

Thanks to her will and courage, Sonia had overcome her fear.

But how many children are afraid to go home alone? There are many. And all of them should know that the journey home from school is not dangerous if all the rules are respected, namely:

- Do not talk to strangers
- Go straight home without stopping
- Be very, very careful when crossing the street
- Always walk on the sidewalk
- Do not trust people you have never seen before.

Sonia learned this after days of terror and now comes home alone every day, full of happiness.

Failure In Mathematics

"I'm never doing math again! In fact, I'm not going to school anymore!" Matilde shouted to her mother.

The little girl, who was in her last year of elementary school, had just received a bad grade in math from which she could not recover.

Matilde was not one of those apathetic, disinterested girls in school. She got good grades and always worked hard for her studies.

For this reason, she could not understand how it was possible not only to not get a good grade but also not to get a "pass" on the last class test!

"Mom, I swear I studied, I don't know why I was so lame," the little girl said tearfully. "Honey, first of all, don't use the word 'suck', because it's not appropriate. And don't worry, all of us, even the teachers, know that you are still studying. A slip-up can happen."

Matilda was confused. If she had studied, why would she fail?

"The teacher doesn't like me! That's why she gave me a bad grade," she said. "But don't talk nonsense. The teacher loves you all and if she gave you that bad grade, it's only because you must have done something wrong."

"I don't know, Mom. In fact, I only know now that I don't want to go to school anymore," she said firmly. "Mati, you have to understand that life's difficulties are not to be avoided but to be faced. Now you have this problem, which is a failure. Do you think that not going to school will solve the problem?"

Matilde hesitated for a moment and then answered, "Yes because I'm sure I won't take anymore." "So you admit that you haven't studied? Since you're thinking of taking more."

"What are you talking about? I'm studying! And I'll never take it again!" the little girl says proudly.

"I believe you, Mati. But you have to prove it. As soon as the next tests come around, you will surely pass and get good grades again. Remember: difficulties must be faced."

"Okay mom, but the next time I fail, I won't go to school. Okay?" asked "No, not okay. It is okay to make mistakes, even more than once. I am an adult now, and I make mistakes every day, what should I do? Should I never leave the house again?

It's not the mistakes you make that count, it's the number of times you try to make up for them. So, it's time for you to make up for it, how about that?"

"Okay, mom, I'll try. But I can't guarantee anything." said Matilde almost sadly. "We believe in you, don't worry, baby."

After a few weeks, the teacher proposed a new math test to the class. Matilde was very nervous but, at the same time, she wanted to prove her true worth.

She was the first to hand in the paper with the assignment. She was satisfied, but quickly remembered that also last time she thought she had done everything correctly.

The days following the audit result were endless. Matilda was anxious to know the result.

So, on the following Monday, the teacher announced the grades: Matilde had obtained the best mark.

She came home full of joy and rushed to hug her mother. "Mom! I got the best grade! I made it up!"

"I had no doubt, honey, you were always fantastic."

"Even when I failed? "

"Of course, you were because you immediately reacted and for that, you are a great person.

Matilde had learned the lesson that nothing is lost as long as you try to do better.

She compensated for her failure by studying even harder, and the positive results came immediately.

For Matilda, it was a lesson that would serve her well for the rest of her life.

If you hav

please contact us by e-mail, and we will send you

the images to print and color.

info.bookebook@gmail.com

When the whole world seems to be against you, always remember that you are special and that no one else in the world is like you.

I hope I've made you understand the importance of being unique. Tell us what you think by writing a review on Amazon.

The Giraffe

Kids Playing In The Rain

Manufactured by Amazon.ca
Bolton, ON

30593292R00048